ATTENTION
OBAMA
HATERS:

What if the Bible is true?
Will your hate of this man be worth the price
you may have to pay?

Annette Boyd Lee

ATTENTION OBAMA HATERS:

What if the Bible is true?
Will your hate of this man be worth the price
you may have to pay?

Annette Boyd Lee

JASHER PRESS & CO.

CONTENTS

Dedication

To God be the glory for the great things He has done!

To my mother, my heart, my love—the late Mrs. Annie Lee Boyd Tate

I miss you, Mama. My tears haven't stopped. My life isn't the same without you. The pain is sometimes unbearable. I long for our moments. But you taught me to trust God, so I must heed your loving advice.

You were so proud to have voted for President Obama. You wanted to meet the President in person. You sat in a wheelchair in a hotel lobby in Asheville, NC, for six hours hoping to meet him. When you didn't get to see him, you were still alright, and proud you had voted for him.

You watched him give speeches on TV. You prayed for him and his family. You never got to see him in person, but I'm sure his thanks and appreciation to the millions included you.

Acknowledgment

To my truly beloved sister: Elder Cynthia Crutchfield

You are the person I know I can count on here on this earth—not because you tell me what I want to hear all the time, but because you tell me what I need to hear. The bond that exists between us is unbreakable.

To my brother-in-law, Lorenzo Crutchfield

We've come a long way, and I thank God for the growth. I love you for loving my sister.

To my spiritual Family, Bishop (Dr.) Kent and First Lady (Dr.) Diana Branch

I thought I was special when you told me that you loved me, your spiritual daughter. But then you showed me with your consistent Biblical teaching, guidance, and correction. That's the love I have longed for. That's the love of a true Spirit-filled man and woman of God. The void has been filled. Thank you.

To the Pilgrim Cathedral of Atlanta Church Family

Driving to church each Sunday isn't a burden because I know, beyond a shadow of a doubt, that when I get there, I will be blessed to be with all of you in the Holy Ghost-filled atmosphere as we receive the Rhema Word. I love you all.

To my family, friends, and foes in my hometown of Clinton, South Carolina

We should never forget where we come from or where we return. The spiritual foundation in my life took root at the Hebron Baptist Church and Mount Cowell Baptist Church. We honor God and those who had an impact on my upbringing and spiritual growth. Thank you and I love you.

Chapter 1

Introduction: A Shameful State of Affairs

Who would have ever thought we would have an African-American president?

In 2008, millions of us proudly supported Barack Obama to become the first African-American president. He made promises he intended to keep. He made declarations he intended to uphold. But every time someone genuinely tries to do the right thing for the right reasons for more people than not, the devil is always busy. What a shameful state of affairs.

We are in a time when it seems that lies are stronger than truth. We get it. The Republicans have banked on the committed Obama supporters being silent. They've banked on the 2008 Obama supporters sitting back while they bashed our President, called him every nasty name possible, and challenged his credentials to be our President. They've made up so many lies and half-truths about what our President set out to do that many people fell for the lies and distortions. The Republicans succeeded in the elections of 2010 and have already shown they intend to keep those same people at bay and continue lying and deceiving. But I believe there will be a big surprise in 2012.

We're watching and paying attention. The Republicans have shown they have access to trillions of dollars–but the truth is free. We don't need to put up ads of lies, deceit, and downright hate. We'll stand with our President and show just how much power truth has over money.

This time, I don't believe the Obama supporters will wait until just before the elections to stand up for our President. We are fired and ready to go–now!

MR. PRESIDENT, DON'T BACK DOWN. BACK THEM UP!!! WE'VE GOT YOU.

Therefore put on the full armor of God, so that when the day of evil comes, you may be able to stand your ground, and after you have done everything, to stand. Stand firm then, with the belt of truth buckled around your waist, with the breastplate of righteousness in place, and with your feet fitted with the readiness that comes from the gospel of peace. Ephesians 6:13-15

Stand, Mr. President! Stand!

Chapter 2

Are you influenced by ungodly counsel?

If the Bible is true, and one day we'll all have to stand at judgment and give account of everything we've said and done, are there any people who'll find themselves weighed in unfavorably in the balance of God's righteous justice because of the feelings they harbored against the President of the United States, Barack Obama?

> *For it is written, as I live, saith the Lord, every knee shall bow to me, and every tongue shall confess to God. So then every one of us shall give account of himself to God. Let us not therefore judge one another anymore: but judge this rather, that no man put a stumbling block or an occasion to fall in his brother's way.* Romans 14:11-13 (KJV)

Make no mistake about it—I don't have a heaven or hell to put anyone in, and I'm not the judge of anyone. But how people can say and do some of the things they've said and done in the political field in the past four years has been amazing to me. Even in the past four years, history has been referenced enough to indicate this type of behavior and attacks have been going on for years. However, history hasn't supported the hatred towards a president as it has been surfaced with the election of President Barack Obama. If you don't believe the Bible is true, nothing in this book should bother you at all. But if you do believe the Bible is true, please consider the impact of what's in your heart with regard to President Barack Obama—and the ultimate penalty or reward you'll receive as a result.

I was once guilty of the quick response to someone trying to correct me on an issue in my life as "You can't judge me," or the Bible says, "Judge not." But thanks to the Word of God being truly manifested in my life, I was convicted by the Word to understand that teaching people about the righteousness of God isn't judging. If a person feels condemnation as a result of the Word of God being shared, then bring on the self-evaluation. With regard to this book and the intent, the above Scripture makes it plain—no man put a stumbling block or an occasion to fall in his brother's way.

If you've lived a life for the Lord—professing love for all God's people, giving as the Bible indicates, and showing charity to the less fortunate—can you now afford to gamble with your salvation? Has the 2008 election of the nation's first African-American president jeopardized your eternal destiny because now you think—or you've been led to believe—the president is some awful person who's been sent to destroy this country?

To thine own self be true. Regardless how hard you

14

may try to fool man, God knows the true heart of every man. This isn't about disagreeing with the President on political issues, or even the running of this nation. Rather, this is a case of pure hatred towards a man and his family for personal reasons. If God had wanted us to agree with everything man did all the time, He would've made us all the same. He made us the same only in His image. We're free-spirited individuals who, in most cases, are capable of making our own decisions in life. What we choose is our responsibility and, ultimately, our judgment with the Lord.

Why write this book? To help someone—anyone—who has fallen in this rut of hatred at the advice of ungodly counsel. *Ungodly counsel?* What am I talking about? I believe those who promote hatred in any form, and have an audience to convince others to participate in this hatred, are proponents of ungodly counsel. To follow these people is to gamble with your salvation—but only if the Bible is true.

> *Blessed is the man that walketh not in the counsel of the ungodly, nor standeth in the way of sinners, nor sitteth in the seat of the scornful. But his delight is in the law of the Lord, and in his law doth he meditate day and night.* Psalm 1:1-2 (KJV)

> *For the Lord knoweth the way of the righteous: but the way of the ungodly shall perish.* Psalm 1:6 (KJV)

I believe many of the people who are easily persuaded by the ungodly counsel may not understand how following such advice would be viewed by God. The emphasis here is on how we should live and treat others. We must take responsibility for the choices we make and ensure that our source of influence has the right motive.

15

Make no mistake about it—those sources of ungodly counsel won't be with you on Judgment Day. That's the work of the devil. His job is to lead people away from God. If people can be taught to hate and not realize that the hate is wrong, Satan has accomplished what he set out to do.

> *The thief cometh not, but for to steal, and to kill, and to destroy: I am come that they might have life, and that they might have it more abundantly.* John 10:10 (KJV)

Who is the thief? The thief is anyone who can influence you to make decisions that are contrary to the Word of God. The thief finds comfort in setting people up. He's savvy in the way he deceives you.

Consider, for example, that the first approach of the thief was to paint the picture that President Obama was anti-American. Of all the people who would be proud to be an American and love this country, I believe President Obama is at the top of the list. His story is compelling. Yet, we find people using this 'talking point' to get people to think otherwise.

There was so much emphasis placed on the President being a Muslim. When the attacks occurred on September 11, 2001, wasn't it President Bush who made the statements concerning the Muslims in this country being a part of this country? The following is an excerpt from a transcript of President Bush's comments at a Washington mosque on September 17, 2001:

> *Both Americans, our Muslim friends and citizens, tax-paying citizens, and Muslim in nations were just appalled and could not*

16

believe what we saw on our TV screens. These acts of violence against innocents violate the fundamental tenets of the Islamic faith, and it's important for my fellow Americans to understand that. The English translation is not as eloquent as the original Arabic, but let me quote from the Quran itself: "In the long run, evil in the extreme will be the end of those who do evil, for that they rejected the signs of Allah and held them up to ridicule." The face of terrorist is not the true faith of Islam. That's not what Islam is all about. Islam is peace. These terrorists don't represent peace, they represent evil and war. When we think of Islam, we think of a faith that brings comfort to a billion people around the world. Billions of people find comfort and solace and peace. And that's made brothers and sisters out of every race, out of every race. America counts millions of Muslims amongst our citizens, and Muslims make an incredibly valuable contribution to our country.

When President Bush spoke these words, there wasn't any of the hatred towards him then as it is being channeled towards our first African-American President.

Then, to make certain that association was viewed as a "cause to fear," the thief made continuous reference to the terrorists. Some have even gone so far as to refer to President Obama as a terrorist. Shame on anyone who would dare refer to him as such.

When the health care debate started, the thief painted the picture that he was going to "kill Grandma." I find it heartbreaking that the Republicans would use talking points to 'scare' the elderly people into thinking President Obama would support any legislature that would purposely harm anyone.

Then there was the issue of his birthplace. I just loved the way people would say, "I know he wasn't born here." Really? Were you there? Was his mother's side of the family such "prophets" that they were able to see that Barack Obama would one day be President? Did they actually fake his birth certificate and all the news articles in Hawaii? Insane, isn't it? That's what the thief is great at.

If the Republicans can get just a few seniors to 'be concerned' about President Obama using all the factors mentioned above, they should be able to secure the votes they need to elect a Republican in 2012. The lies are running rampart, even now. I have seen some of the emails and it is hate propaganda for sure. If you don't know God for yourself, and you have no discernment in your ability to see through such lies and distortions and can't make decisions for yourself, then you could be easily persuaded to believe everything that has been made up about President Obama.

The Bible is an instrument of:

1) Direction.

   a. It directs us how to treat others.

   And the second is like, namely this, "Thou shalt love thy neighbour as thyself. There is none other commandment greater than these." Mark 12:31 (KJV)

Remind the people to be subject to rulers and authorities, to be obedient, to be ready to do whatever is good, to slander no one, to be peaceable and considerate, and to show true humility toward all men. Titus 3:1-2

If the Bible is true, how can a person declare by mouth that they're a Christian and publicly display so many hateful and dishonest tactics for the sake of winning a political race? The Word of God teaches us to love our neighbors as well as our enemies. I'm not talking about enemies abroad, but those here in our country, our communities, and our neighborhoods.

What kind of country would we be if we fought as hard to love one another as some do to hate one another? Even if you don't believe in the Bible—if you read it simply as a book of stories about people in the times of the Bible—what's wrong with the principles of how to treat people?

But the fruit of the Spirit is love, joy, peace, patience, kindness, goodness, faithfulness, gentleness, and self-control. Against such things there is no law. Those who belong to Christ Jesus have crucified the sinful nature with its passions and desires. Since we live by the Spirit, let us keep in step with the Spirit. Let us not become conceited, provoking and envying each other. Galatians 5:22-26

Why do so many people reject any form of direction that seeks to make life better for everyone? Why, instead, do so many people incite hatred?

Consider, if you will, an internal inventory of the contents of your heart. Sit down and draw the shape of a heart on a piece of paper and use the following colors to fill the heart—blue for love, green for jealousy, and red for hatred. (You can add your own colors)

What color would be the predominate color in your heart? We can say we love everyone, but that doesn't mean it's true. If you only get one point from this book, take this one. God knows our thoughts before we think them. He knows our actions before we do them. He knows the true content of our hearts.

b. It directs us how to live this life, even with the trials and tribulations, so that our ultimate results will be that of salvation and eternal life.

> They said to you, "In the last times, there will be scoffers who will follow their own ungodly desires." These are the men who divide you, who follow mere natural instincts and do not have the Spirit. But you, dear friends, build yourselves up in your most holy faith and pray in the Holy Spirit. Keep yourselves in God's love as you wait for the mercy of our Lord Jesus Christ to bring you to eternal life.
> Jude 18-21

Everything we need to live a good life is found in the Bible. When we have trouble in our lives and/or the lives of family and friends, God's Word is our source of solutions. His Word can be trusted. It'll never steer us in the wrong direction. This isn't true of the ungodly counsel that lurks the airwaves—and even some churches.

2) Correction.

    a. It corrects us when we are wrong.

All Scripture is given by inspiration of God, and is profitable for doctrine, for reproof, for correction, for instruction in righteousness.
II Timothy 3:16 (KJV)

If the Bible is true, the correction that is given by the Word of God is for our good. When God inspired Paul to write these words, he was given incite to our disobedient tendency to not follow the Word of God. Unfortunately for some of us, our free will overrides our ability to be totally faithful. Even when we purposely and diligently try to live a Christian life, we fall short. This is where grace and mercy intercedes on our behalf.

Today we have access to the Word of God in a variety of different formats. There are numerous translations of the Bible available which provides clarity of the verses. Also, there are many Biblical scholars who have written references for all sorts of issues we face in our lives. No one has to search the Scriptures independently for answers. With the availability of the Internet, no one should say they can't find the answers they need in the Scriptures.

    b. It corrects us when we are going in the wrong direction.

He who heeds discipline shows the way to life, but whoever ignores correction leads others astray. He who conceals his hatred has lying lips, and whoever spreads slander

21

is a fool. Proverbs 10:17-18

A man who remains stiff-necked after many rebukes will suddenly be destroyed—without remedy. When the righteous thrive, the people rejoice; when the wicked rule, the people groan. Proverbs 29:1-2

There's a key element to the direction and correction in the Bible. You've got to want it! You've got to want to live a life that's pleasing to God and lines up with his Word. Unfortunately, if people don't believe in God and/or the Bible, they will develop their own form of guidance or leisure. If the Bible is true, we'll have the privilege of a private meeting with God one day whereby He'll give us opportunity to clear up any misunderstanding during our lifetime. Unfortunately, to wait until that time comes won't change the destination of anyone who hadn't live for Christ in their earthly existence.

Chapter 3

Why is President Obama despised and hated so much?

Is it the color of his skin? If yes, why? Doesn't he represent by his heritage both the white and African-American races? Most white people won't own a mixed-race person as part of their race. Most of us African-American people love this bi-racial person.

Is there a fear out there that has been perpetrated by the enemy to scare some of the white voters—especially the elderly—that the "blacks are going to take over"? Why do people of any race have to "take over"? Why can't we all be a part of the human race? If that's the route the enemy wants to take, consider this Scripture.

> *But many who are first will be last; and many who are last will be first.* Matthew 19:30

Notice the Bible didn't say all that are first shall be last. It said many. Thankfully, not everyone falls for the tricks of the enemy. It wasn't just the African-Americans who voted President Obama into office. He appealed to all races of people as demonstrated by the rallies during his campaign.

There's a change taking place in the ethnicity in the United States. We have another race of people that's growing rapidly—the Hispanics. Then there are the mixed races of people. Will these people be as despised and rejected as President Obama has been as they become more prominent in the U.S. society?

One would think that we, the people of the United States, would've stood together to celebrate the progress that was made in our racial discord with President Obama's election. Instead of embracing the election as a positive move towards equality; the election, seemingly, has unleashed a fury of hatred that hasn't been seen in years.

Is it because he is intelligent, handsome, smart, and articulate? If yes, why? Would you rather have some unknowledgeable, uneducated, baggy-pants-below-the-waist individual speaking on behalf of the United States? The man has demonstrated he can stand with the best of them. He is simultaneously down-to-earth and upper-class. With superb dialect, he can talk to people of all levels, races, and religious beliefs.

Do not hate your brother in your heart. Rebuke your neighbor frankly so you will not share in his guilt. Leviticus 19:17

Understand that the Word of God is clear. Hatred is not an area whereby we who profess to be Christians should be associated. Hatred is a heavy burden to carry and it is self-inflicted. President Obama has not demonstrated hatred towards anyone. Therefore, the haters have actually given him power over their emotions.

Is it because he is a devoted family man? If yes, why? When society constantly emphasizes the number of African-American men who are incarcerated or deadbeat dads, shouldn't we be excited to have a faithful family man representing the United States? My heart goes out to his family for having to be subjected to so many personal attacks.

Anyone who hates his brother is a murderer, and you know that no murderer has eternal life in him. I John 3:15

To hate a person is a very serious issue—only if the Bible is true. The Word of God doesn't mince words. This isn't about not liking his policies and what he's doing as President. It's about that harbored feeling of hatred toward this man personally. To hate a person has be continuous work; if only a person could get paid for it. We would have a few short term millionaires everywhere.

Is it because YOU think he doesn't know enough to be President? Remember—the key phrase is YOU think. Most of us don't know the full details of any issue that the President has to address on a daily basis. More importantly, if YOU are honest about the situation, you'll acknowledge that President Obama, while a candidate, repeatedly said he would make mistakes, there would be false starts, things would take time, and other comments to that effect. That alone told me he was a man of integrity. I remember on the campaign trail that he was greatly criticized for his "lack of experience" to be president. Just who has experience being a President? Former Presidents.

People said he didn't know enough about the

military to be a good commander-in-chief. He was good enough to command the killing of Osama Bin Laden. He's a decision-maker. He listens to people, but ultimately he's the one who makes the decisions. Once he makes the decisions, he owns them. If the President was making every decision without the input of anyone, I'd be the first to say the man isn't a good leader. But I believe that by his actions, he seeks counsel and works hard to make the best decision in the best interest of ALL the American people. He doesn't run around blaming other people for the problems within his own administration. He took the oath and, I believe, he represents the epitome of a real commander.

A commander is responsible for what his troops do and fail to do. That was a saying used extensively in the Army. I believe it's an exemplified position President Obama adopted when he became President. "Yes, but he's been blaming the Bush administration," you may say. The Bush administration is responsible for most of the current economic condition the country faces now. Just because the Republicans are saying over and over again that President Obama has increased the debt by trillions of dollars—and that's why we're in the recession now—doesn't make it the whole truth. Yes, the debt has increased. What the Republicans aren't making clear is that the stimulus was put in place to boost the economy—and it has. It hasn't boosted the economy to the extent the President wanted, but it has kept us from an all-out depression. The Republican politicians know this to be the truth. But if you knew it, their lies and distortions would be revealed.

Take the automotive industry. How many people are working now because of the bailout to GM? If the Republicans had had their way, those jobs would've been lost. They didn't want GM to be helped. Can *these* people be considered anti-American if they would rather sabotage the economy than support programs that actually help the economy, which then speaks positively of the President's accomplishments? Seriously, can we call the President anti-American while he is working to get this country moving at the perils of a Republican party who refuses to make necessary changes in spending cuts and revenue increases? Who is really going against—*anti* the progress of this country to help the people *–American*?

Thank God there are some rich Republicans who now believe they should do more. Mr. Ken Langone, Vantis Capital Management Chairman, made the following statement:

> *"We've got to take some pain. Well, I say this as a devout Republican. I think in these negotiations, I think, #1, guys like me, I've said this before. But there is a caveat. I shouldn't get Social Security. I should pay more taxes. But all the money generated out of those actions should be entirely devoted to paying down debt."*

Then there was Mr. Alan Greenspan who said:

> *"I think that the Republicans ought to identify a very significant amount of so-called tax expenditures, which, in fact, are misclassified. They are expenditures, they are outlays, and many of them are subsidies, and subsidies are not the type of things that you want for an efficient market system."*

> *"My view is this: I was in favor of the Bush*

27

tax cuts on the grounds that it was the dissipation of a surplus. As soon as it became obvious that the surplus disappeared, I no longer supported that. And my view about taxes is that I would like them as low as possible, but not with borrowed money."

To God be the Glory! Mr. Langone, Mr. Greenspan—your words were refreshing. Thank you. While some people in your own party may take exception to what you said, I believe God is pleased with your honesty about this situation. I'm sure there are more rich people who would be willing to go back to the pre-Bush tax rates because they know the taxes wouldn't hurt them financially.

I wonder why those tax cuts weren't automatically repealed when the surplus was gone. Why wasn't Congress fiscally responsible when the deficit started rising? GREED—that's why. Are you still not convinced that the Republicans will sabotage the well-being of the country for the sake of making this President look bad in hopes he won't be re-elected in 2012?

It seems that maybe there are a few millionaires and billionaires in the United States who don't support the position the Republicans are taking right now. TO GOD BE THE GLORY!

Chapter 4

2008 supporters: We don't need to straddle the fence.

W hen then-Senator Obama was campaigning and inspiring so many people, he won the election because so many supported him then. But now, some seem to want to turn their back on him.

Why? He hasn't done what he said he would do? Yes, he has—to the best of his ability considering all the opposition he has been dealing with on everything he has done. If you take the time to listen to the facts, you'll understand that President Obama wanted to do all he said in the campaign. I believe the reality of the situation is that the very night he won the election; the "Stop this man from succeeding" message became the number-one objective of the Republicans. At first, it was being said quietly. Then, the more the President appeared to be making progress; the objective began to be voiced openly.

Take, for example, South Carolina Senator DeMint's Waterloo comment on health care. Why would a Senator fight so hard to prevent people in his own state from having health care benefits? Maybe he'd say it's because it would bankrupt the U.S.? Really? What about those tax breaks for the people who don't need tax cuts—the rich? I wonder how many millions of dollars the millionaires spent to keep from paying an extra $100,000 per year in taxes. Mr./Ms. Millionaire/Billionaire, just how much do you need? You can't take it with you. If you have been blessed enough or ruthless enough to acquire millions or billions, do you really think God would penalize you for paying the taxes which you haven't had to pay in the last ten years?

Note: Tonight, I'm sitting here listening to Congressman Eric Cantor stand boldly and declare that the Senate Majority Leader, Harry Reid, shouldn't stop the repeal of the health care bill from being voted on in the Senate. He shouldn't let a bill fall dead when the "American people" have spoken. Excuse me—wasn't it these same people who held up many bills that passed through the House in the 111th Congress that some of these same Republicans wouldn't let a vote be taken in the Senate? How many times did they filibuster? It turns out the vote was a good thing because it identified those in Congress who were willing to vote against allowing the American people to have guaranteed health care—even with pre-existing conditions.

This double standard has to be about lying so much that the lie is believed to be the truth. If they say a lie enough times, the gullible will believe it to be true—especially if they already harbor hate towards the person or thing about which the lie is being told.

Let me try to clear up something about the tax cut issues. The Republicans are trying to paint the picture that President Obama is going to raise taxes on everybody.

THAT IS NOT TRUE. The Republicans get on the news outlets and radio and repeatedly make the statement that no one should raise taxes on the American people during a recession. THAT IS NOT WHAT THE PRESIDENT IS DOING. The President and the Democrats have repeatedly said the tax increase is only for those making over $250,000 a year. That number has fluctuated some, and by the time this book is published, it may be more or less.

This isn't an issue for people making less than $250,000. Ask yourself—do you make more than $250,000 a year? If not, this particular discussion about raising taxes doesn't apply to you. We have people in the United States who have paid fewer taxes than millions of people making less than $100,000 per year. These people are the millionaires and billionaires. If you're in the middle- or low-income bracket, your taxes will NOT increase under the plan being proposed by President Obama and the Democrats.

When President Bush entered his first year as President, we didn't have a deficit issue. There was a surplus. Over the next eight years, the surplus became a huge deficit. The deficit didn't occur in one term. It occurred over an eight-year period. Was the deficit actually higher than it appeared because the two unfunded wars weren't included in the deficit calculation under the Bush Administration? So why do people really think President Obama and his administration can reverse this situation in three years? Let's get personal. If a person gains weight continuously over an eight-year period and wakes up one day and realizes he weighs over 300 pounds, the healthy way to lose the weight is a slow process whereby the person's lifestyle changes. To drop a quick pound here and there leads to the recurrence of weight gain. Only when the person accepts that they must make a

31

conscientious decision to change their lifestyle will they be able to shed those pounds reasonably without harming their health. I use this illustration because most people can understand the weight problem that exists in this country.

The deficit issue of the United States is somewhat similar. The government took a huge surplus and, over an eight-year period, turned it into an enormous deficit. No one in their right mind should even think it's practical to reverse the financial crisis that exists today in a four-year period—especially when the people's party who instigated this catastrophe is doing everything they can to sabotage the efforts of the President.

Is this not the United States of America? United, being the operative word. I know there are those who have spoken boldly of seceding from the union. Unless that becomes a reality, shouldn't we seek to work together for the common good?

Behold, how good and how pleasant it is for brethren to dwell together in unity? Psalm 133:1

Chapter 5

The Christian Conservative

During the past four years, I've listened to some of the most outrageous comments from politicians and political commentators. One of the most amazing things to me is the use of the words "Christian conservatives" when describing some politicians who profess to be Christians.

A Christian is supposed to be Christ-like—so I've been taught. Yet, by some of their words and deeds, these politicians in no way exemplify a Christ-like demeanor. Take Mr. "You lie," for example. Screaming at the President of the United States in the manner that he did the night of the State of the Union in 2010 was, without a doubt, totally disrespectful—not only to the President, but also to the American people. The President didn't lie. If this Congressman is a "Christian conservative," why would he yell that way? Consider the possibility that by doing so, he would gain instantaneous fame—and he did. Everyone wanted to know who said it, and by the time the President's address was over, Congressman's Wilson's identity was known. What happened after that? He raised a lot of money.

If this outburst was an example of bearing false witness, why would the people support such an action? Hatred is one reason. It seems that the Obama haters aren't concerned about the truth in the political arena. They only want the hate towards the President in hopes of preventing his re-election.

The following part was written June 30, 2011, in response to Senator John Cornyn from Texas, who stood on the Senate floor and attacked the President's speech:

> *"This is a grand opportunity for Democrats and Republicans to come together to do the nation's business, to be serious. Not to be reckless, not to give demagogic speeches like the President gave yesterday as a part of his reelection campaign. Absolutely disgraceful. He should be ashamed. I respect the office of the President of the United States, but I think the President has diminished that office and himself by giving the kind of campaign speeches that he gave yesterday."*

Demagogic – Characteristic of a demagogue (one who tries to stir up the people by appeals to emotion, prejudice, etc., in order to become a leader and accomplish selfish ends)

Disgraceful – causing or characterized by disgrace (a being in disfavor because of bad conduct, etc., loss of respect, public dishonor, shame. A person or thing that brings shame (to one))

Ashamed – feeling shame (a person or thing that brings dishonor)

For those of you reading this book who aren't familiar with the line, "I respect the office of the President of the United States," what he's actually saying is, "I respect the office, but not the man." People would do this all the time in the military by starting a statement with, "With all due respect to your rank, Sir…" That is a blatant statement of disrespect to the person being addressed.

Senator, with all due (no, I won't go there), the first part of your statement was very good. But after "reckless," you, sir, became "absolutely disgraceful." The Republican politicians absolutely hate the fact that this man can stand up to them. When President Obama met with the Republicans on health care and the cameras were there, his calm and positive demeanor was no match for them. *How dare this black man talk to us white men like that!*

I was in a discussion when a statement was made that these politicians have been in power for so long that they cannot accept the fact that we have an African-American president. The long-term politicians have been in control for so long and have been setting the United States up for private takeover for years. All of a sudden, there is an election of an African-American who is not part of their takeover objective. Needless to say, this is a serious problem for those who had anticipated being in control of what takes place in the government.

We keep hearing the Republicans say they want to make certain the government stays out of our personal business. Do people really understand what that mean? If the government does not have oversight on food regulations, companies would be able to prepare and sell food with little to no safety measures. Imagine getting some meat that hasn't been thoroughly processed. Would you be concerned about the contamination of that product before it ever made it to your dinner table? The reason we have recall is because companies are required to monitor it's product to ensure standards are maintained.

Wasn't it just a year ago (2010) leading up to the elections that the Republicans and Tea Party were promoting demagogic behavior in the town hall meetings against the Democrats? Senator Cornyn, did you stand up and say that was unacceptable? That was disgraceful. Those people should've been ashamed. When the members of Congress were spit at going into the building, what was that about? It was about hate—plain and simple.

Who were the demagogues then?

Then there is the issue with some churches promoting hatred. I thought the church was supposed to spread the good news of Jesus Christ. Yet there are many churches that have taken on a political platform and are teaching hatred from the pulpit. What is coming out of your church? We saw during the campaign that then-Senator Obama's church came under attack by the right. Is anyone calling out the white churches that are doing the same thing? Many churches and ministries are openly using their platforms to teach and preach hatred toward President Obama. They are using those 'scare tactics' in their wording to convince the people President Obama is 'out to get you.' If our black churches were doing that, the government would be there to threaten to take their tax-exempt status.

If anyone says, "I love God," yet hates his brother, he is a liar. For anyone who does not love his brother, whom he has seen, cannot love God, whom he has not seen. And he has given us this command: Whoever loves God must also love his brother. I John 4:20-21

It's what's in your heart that matters.

Do not store up for yourselves treasures on earth, where moth and rust destroy, and where thieves break in and steal. But store up for yourselves treasures in heaven, where moth and rust do not destroy, and where thieves do not break in and steal. For where your treasure is, there your heart will be also. Matthew 6:19-21

Again, it's what's in the heart that matters.

Chapter 6

Mr. President: Thank you. Secretary Clinton: I apologize.

While I cannot speak for anyone else, I can give an example of how President Obama's demeanor and decision to campaign positively gave me something to think about.

I recall going to Lander University in Greenwood, SC, to hear then-Senator Obama on the campaign trail. In preparing for this short drive, I sat at my computer and came up with a sign that was negative in nature towards Mrs. Clinton. I don't remember what it said, but when I arrived at the event, the hand-sized signs were taken from me. "Why?" I asked, annoyed. The answer was simple. Then-Senator Obama didn't want anything negative to be portrayed at his rallies. "But I'm on your side, Senator Obama. I want you to win," I thought. While I wanted the sign to show my support for him, I failed to understand, until that day, the type of person President Obama is. Shame on me.

I'll take a short break to say to Secretary Clinton, "I apologize. Sincerely, I apologize." Regardless of how much I wanted then-Senator Obama to win, being negative towards his opponent wasn't the way to show my support. When then-Senator Clinton accepted the position as Secretary of State, she fed me a piece of humble pie. Mrs. Clinton, it takes a tough lady to be able to overcome the heartaches of the campaign and still be a sincere player. *You're the best.*

On the campaign trail, they both fought a hard fight. They both stirred the emotions of millions in this election who hadn't been involved in politics. I canvassed for Senator Obama—not only in my community, but also in Charlotte, NC. That was a first for me. There was so much passion in place for these two candidates. With my poor judgment in wanting to use the sign, I was taught humility by the excellent Obama campaign resolve not to stoop to the disgraceful level of the rallies of the other party.

After then-Senator Obama won the Democratic nomination, the outburst of hate became overwhelming. After he won the Presidency, the hate became deafening. Tea Party rallies popped up all over the United States.

There was a time when racism and hatred weren't so commonly and openly displayed. But now, even children are put at the forefront of hatred. Why would a parent have his child out in public displaying hate signs? The child was not born with hate in his heart. The parent was certainly planting that seed.

> *Train up a child in the way he should go, and when he is old, he will not depart from it.* Proverbs 22:6 (KJV)

By choice, this parent has set the stage for his child to learn hate at a young age. When he gets old enough to make his own decisions, he'll not only harbor hate within; but he'll most likely follow in his parent's footsteps and teach his children the concept of hate for political and/or personal reasons. To this child, this behavior has to be right because Mommy/Daddy taught him how to do it.

When a group of "supporters" shows up at a rally with derogatory signs, pictures, and chants, what does it say for the campaign they are "supporting" when the leaders in that rally not only fail to denounce the signs, pictures, and chants, but actually participate in them? How can they say with a straight face that what they represent, support, and allow is indicative of a leader who would be for ALL the people of the United States?

If the Bible is real and true, how will these people justify to God how they've acted, what they've said, and, more importantly, how they've harbored such hatred in their hearts?

Be not deceived; God is not mocked; for whatsoever a man soweth, that shall he also reap. Galatians 6:7 (KJV)

What are the politicians and commentators reaping?

How wrong is it to use lies and distortions to get people to support a campaign? What does it say about the people who would believe the lies and jump on the bandwagon of misguided support? If an argument was made based on the truth—the whole truth—I wouldn't have an issue here. But the problem exists because of the way the talking points are used—buzz words to get the vulnerable to listen, feed their politically-driven fear and hatred, and agree with the point being made. On the surface, this may be excellent for the politician. But in the long run, if the Bible is true, will they reap the wrath of God's judgment for the deception?

Take, for example, the health care bill. The bill that President Obama signed was called "The Affordable Health Care Act." The bill has been renamed by the Republicans as "Obamacare" and "The Job Killing Health Care Bill." Why would a "Christ-like" politician have to lie about a bill that was approved to help millions of people live? Why would they have such contempt for the "least of them?" This one is dangerous, because if the Bible is true, those who have participated in this deception have done more than just deceive the people.

> *And the King shall answer and say unto them, Verily I say unto you, Inasmuch as ye have done it unto one of the least of these my brethren, ye have done it unto me.* Matthew 25:40 (KJV)

> *But the fearful, and unbelieving, and the abominable, and murderers, and whoremongers, and sorcerers, and idolaters, and all liars, shall have their part in the lake which burneth with fire and brimstone, which is the second death.* Revelations 21:8 (KJV)

During the health care debate, I received an email from the Obama administration asking me to write my Congressman and tell him to support the health care bill. I did, by email, and to my surprise, I received a letter from Congressman Jeff Duncan.

Mr. President: Thank you. Secretary Clinton: I apologize.

Here is the content of Congressman Duncan's letter to me (dated February 4, 2011):

Dear Ms. Lee,

Thank you for contacting my office regarding your concerns about health care.

As a fiscal conservative and a firm believer in our Constitution, I could not support the Affordable Care Act. This bill will cost our government billions of dollars and contains an unconstitutional mandate for citizens to buy health insurance. As a result, I voted for the "Repeal of the Job-Killing Health Care Law Act" on January 19th.

Our renewed focus in this new Congress is to get the whole of federal spending reined in. This is our greatest responsibility for today's voters and for future generations who will be saddled with paying down this debt.

In the coming months, the House will be working to draft new legislation to replace the Patient Protect and Affordable Care Act. It is my hope that we can come up with a bipartisan alternative piece of legislation that will better serve our citizens.

As your Representative in Congress, I welcome input from you and all my constituents on health care reform.

Mr. President: Thank you. Secretary Clinton: I apologize.

When bills concerning health care reach the floor this session, I will keep your concerns in mind. Again, thank you for contacting my office.

Sincerely,

(Original Signed)

Jeff Duncan
Member of Congress

Here is the content of my response to his letter (dated February 9, 2011):

At the top of my letterhead was the Prayer of Jabez, as shown below:

> *Oh, that you would bless me indeed, and enlarge my territory, that your hand would be with me, and that you would keep me from evil, **that I may not cause pain**.* I Chronicles 4:10 (NKJV)

Dear Congressman Duncan,

Thank you for the letter dated February 2, 2011, concerning your position on the health care bill. Although I wasn't actually surprised by your position, I was left somewhat puzzled by it. Let me explain.

First of all, you indicated you were a fiscal conservative and a firm believer in the Constitution. I noticed you didn't say you were a Christian conservative. So, as a fiscal conservative, specifically what in the bill makes it such a bad bill? What is so bad in this bill that you, with "sound mind," could vote against something that was established to help so many people? Not only that, specifically how will the bill bankrupt the U.S. as it has been repeatedly said by the Republicans?

Second, specifically, what jobs will the health care bill kill? By the way, isn't that a form of "bearing false witness"? Why do the Republicans use the term "Repeal the Job-Killing Health Care Law Act"? That's not what the bill is called that President Obama signed. Why—if you truly believe it will kill jobs—why couldn't you call it what it is and indicate that you and/or the Republicans believe it will kill jobs?

Third, am I really a constituent of yours? If so, why haven't I or anyone in my family ever heard from you in terms of a meeting or questionnaire on what our needs are in terms of health care? How can you say the people you represent are in agreement with your vote when the people like me can't say you really represent my interest? The Republicans keep saying the American people don't want this bill. Who are **those** American people?

These past two years have been eye-opening for people like me. I have sat back and watched politics like never before, and I

Mr. President: Thank you. Secretary Clinton: I apologize.

am deeply disturbed by the Republican's mannerism when it comes to the issues of the Obama administration. I honestly believe President Obama is a President for ALL the people, whether they accept him or not. I believe the Republicans have been bought with a price (and I am not talking about the Lord) and, as such, you are not representing your constituents, but rather the businesses who you think will keep you in office.

If the next to the last statement in your letter is true and you will keep my concerns in mind, then I will challenge you to do just that. I fear that many of you will bend over backwards to fight against everything President Obama wants to do for ALL the people of the United States. He has been attacked by so many: Mr. "You Lie" from SC, Mr. "Waterloo" from SC, Mr. "He's a Muslim" from all over, Mr. "He Wasn't Born Here" from all over, and so on.

The Republicans created a monster of debt for the United States under the Bush administration. What was your position at that time? Were you a fiscal conservative then?

Mr. Duncan, I don't know you or what you are about as an individual, but from what I see of you in the collective role you play with your Republican counterparts, I don't like and don't feel you are representing me and people like me at all.

Mr. President: Thank you. Secretary Clinton: I apologize.

Please "cause no pain."

Sincerely,

(Original signed)

Annette Lee

There hasn't been any further communication between Congressman Duncan and myself. In his defense, he probably never saw my letter. For the record, I understand that Congressman Duncan is in his first term in Washington.

I submit these letters as examples of how, I believe, the elected officials have lost sight of what their jobs really should be, and how they have fallen into a trap of greed for wealth and power. Ironically, I don't believe every Republican really wants to do all the things they're doing. Rather, I believe they're threatened by the party leaders to the point of non-support if they dare agree with anything the Obama administration puts forward.

How many times has President Obama supported a plan that the Republicans initiated previously, only to have the Republicans go against that same plan simply because President Obama agrees that it's a good idea? The hate is so strong that people can't see what the real objective is.

A double minded man is unstable in all his ways. James 1:8 (KJV)

In the letter from Congressman Duncan, notice the buzz words "unconstitutional" and "job-killing." By using these "talking-point buzz words," they are playing tag with the fear propaganda they started earlier. What's unconstitutional about trying to help people?

47

Mr. President: Thank you. Secretary Clinton: I apologize.

As I write this book, the current dominant political issue is the debt ceiling. This situation is so sad that it's actually funny.

In previous years, raising the debt ceiling hasn't had this much of a problem getting approved. But this year, it is extremely hard because the Republicans "have got to stop all this spending" in order to decrease the deficit.

The President wanted Congress and the Vice-President to work out a deal on the issue of the debt ceiling. The Republicans wanted to cut social entitlements like Social Security and Medicare. The Democrats wanted to increase revenue from the taxes of the rich. The Vice-President was working with Congress to come up with a deal. But the Republicans realized they needed the President involved. They needed to pull him in so they could go on record and blame him.

Note: If the President had come in from the beginning, the Republicans would've said the President wasn't allowing Congress to do their job. After the Republicans pitched a tantrum because the President wasn't with them, he got involved. There was some progress made with the Speaker of the House, Congressman Boehner.

Hold up, wait a minute. Let me put some hate in it. Speaker Boehner was then attacked by his party, so he comes out "strong" that there is no deal even close to being made. Back and forth, back and forth—the situation is so sad that it's actually funny! Mr. President, you can't win with these Republicans no matter what you do.

Lord, I pray someone will see the big picture here

48

Mr. President: Thank you. Secretary Clinton: I apologize.

and truly understand what's at stake if they have been misled to hate.

Chapter 7

The Constitution of the United States of America
versus
The Holy Bible

If the Bible was true before the Constitution was written, has the Bible been superseded by the Constitution? I ask because I keep hearing people refer to their rights in the Constitution. When people make these comments, it seems to me they are identifying the Constitution as the document by which we are to live more than the Bible. For example, the first amendment to the Constitution gives us freedom of speech. But the Bible tells us the tongue is evil, filled with deadly poison, and can't be tamed.

> *But no man can tame the tongue. It is an unruly evil, full of deadly poison.* James 3:8 (NKJV)

Another much-debated issue exists with the 2nd amendment, the right to bear arms. It seems that somewhere in the history of the United States, we've lost the simple principle of love for one another. The Constitution does give us the right to bear arms, but the Bible tells us to pray for one another and live peacefully.

> *Therefore, I exhort, first of all, that supplications, prayers, intercessions, and giving of thanks be made for all men, for kings and all who are in authority, that we may lead a quiet and peaceable life in all godliness and reverence. For this is good and acceptable in the sight of God our Savior, who desires all men to be saved and to come to the knowledge of the truth.* I Timothy 2:1-4 (NKJV)

So, as a Christian, because we have the Constitution, does that mean what we say or how we live is of no consequences when it comes to the Bible?

A lot of people have repeatedly said they want to "take their country back." Back from where? Where did it go? Do you want to take the country back from the African-American president? If anyone has the right to say they want to take their country back, wouldn't it be the Native Americans? There are people who simply don't get it because some ungodly person on the radio or on TV told them what to believe and do. Shame on them.

Consider, if you will, that President Obama is a president of all the people, whether you want him to be or not. When he was on the campaign trail, there were all races present at his rallies. This wasn't so with the Republican campaign. Their campaign consisted of mainly white supporters and people from other races here and there. The things we focus on as a country should be of benefit to all the people—not just a select race or group of people.

Oh my goodness, did a real elected official use the words 'tar baby' in reference to the President of the United States?   Did he exercise his first amendment rights thinking there would be no consequences?   Tea Party Republican   Congressman   Doug   Lamborn,   U.S. Representative for Colorado made this statement.

> *"Even if some people say, 'Well the Republicans should have done this or they should have done that,' they will hold the President responsible. Now, I don't even want to have to be associated with him. It's like touching a tar baby and you get it, you're stuck, and you're a part of the problem now and you can't get away. I don't want that to happen to us, but if it does or not, he'll still get, properly so, the blame because his policies for four years will have failed the American people."*

WOW! Are there any black people in Colorado? I ask this because Representative Lamborn said he didn't realize this had racial connotation. Really, what is tar? Representative Lamborn, I pray you do the right things: pray for forgiveness, ask God to move hatred from your heart and then resign.

It was reported on August 2, 2011, that Representative Lamborn had sent a letter of apology to the President. Then he made the comment,

> *"I absolutely intended no offense, and if this is at all on his radar screen, I am sure that*

he will not take offense and he'll be happy to accept my apology because he is a man of character."

He goes on to say he regrets that he chose the phrase "tar baby,' rather than the word "quagmire."

Quagmire – wet, boggy ground, yielding under the feet. A difficult position, as of one sinking in a quagmire.

Tar – a thick, sticky, brown to black liquid obtained by the destructive distillation of wood, coal, etc.

And the two are the same how? I did find in the Thesaurus for quagmire under predicament (n.) – sticky situation. But I doubt there is anywhere you'd be able to find quagmire with a black connotation as with tar.

So let me get this straight, if a tea party Republican makes a racist comment about the President of the United States, he can fall back on 'I didn't know it had a racial meaning' and that makes everything alright. To my one reader of this book, anytime an 'apology' includes the word 'if' in it, it's not really an apology. When a person really apologizes, they do not use 'if' under any circumstance. Please Congressman Lamborn, go through R&R....Repent and Resign.

To your credit, Congressman Lamborn, you were absolutely correct when you said the President 'is a man of character.' Despite all attempts to provoke him to anger, President Obama continues to maintain his positive demeanor.

Hold up, wait a minute, let me put more hate in it! The very next week after Congressman Lamborn made his statement; Pat Buchanan decided to keep it going by his comment to Reverend Al Sharpton. In discussing whether or not President Obama would extend the Bush tax cuts, Pat Buchanan said,

> *"And let me tell you, your boy, Barack Obama, caved in on it in 2010 and he'll cave in on it again." And he repeated it again. "He's your boy in the ring, he's your fighter."*

Mr. Buchanan, you knew what you were saying when you said it. You also knew the response you would get from Reverend Sharpton.

> *For as he thinks in his heart, so is he. 'Eat and drink!' he says to you, but his heart is not with you.* Proverbs 23:7 (KJV)

Senator Cornyn, how would *you* describe *these* comments from Congressman Lamborn and Pat Buchanan? Should they be ashamed?

> *Then Peter opened his mouth and said; 'In truth I perceive that God shows no partiality. But in every nation whoever fears Him and works righteousness is accepted by Him.* Acts 10:34-35 (KJV)

There is no racial prejudice with the Lord. Consequently, if the Bible is true, people who subscribe to racism and hate will fall short in the sight of the Lord.

We all know this hate, racism and disrespect in

politics can stop. Where are the standards to hold office in the United States of America and represent the American People? The people who are elected officials should be immediately voted out of office for demonstrating and inciting such behavior. If the American People started voting these people out, the behavior in Washington would change drastically. I believe to leave them in office is saying you, the voter, support this behavior and want it to continue. If this is the case, I pray that God will grab your attention by whatever means necessary to save your soul.

Chapter 8

Is God a Socialist?

By the standards of many in the Republican Party, would God be a Socialist? He would be more concerned for the poor and less fortunate people. Therefore, God would seemingly be rejected by those who find it difficult to support legislature for the poor, but have no issue with legislature that continues to benefit the rich.

The answer is no. He would be rejected—but God isn't a Socialist. He is just, and confirmation of His justice can be found in the Bible—His Word—which cuts like a two-edged sword.

He who oppresses the poor shows contempt for their Maker, but whoever is kind to the needy honors God. Proverbs 14:31

I agree there're a lot of problems with spending that need to be addressed. When social programs like Electronic Benefit Transfer (EBT), formally food stamps, and Medicaid were put in place, were they intended to be a way of life for the rest of a person's life? Not at all.

The food stamp program, or EBT. When I was a child, my mother was working in the cotton mill when the work slowed down, and we went on food stamps. I will be the first to admit that we ate well during that time. But as soon as work picked up, my mother got off the food stamps and we went back to eating what she could afford to buy. Many people stayed on food stamps as long as the system allowed them to.

Today, we have people who are grossly taking advantage of this program. The next time you go to a grocery store around the time of a holiday, watch for people who have a buggy filled with hamburger meat, hot dogs, ribs, buns, drinks, etc. Then watch them as they pull out their EBT cards to pay for it. I believe this is abuse of the system. These people are having friends and/or family cookouts at the expense of the system. Why is this allowed? This is an example of where changes need to take place immediately. If people are using the EBT cards, there has to be some record of what they're purchasing. Why isn't there someone monitoring that program for fraud and abuse at the state and/or federal level?

I'm a foster mother and I receive Women, Infant and Children (WIC) support for kids in my care under the age of five. If I tried to get an item that wasn't authorized, it would be rejected at the register. I'm certain that there are items rejected by EBT, such as cigarettes and alcohol, but the abuse may be in the quantity. Maybe the program should be expanded to monitor quantities of a particular item for the month.

I make these examples to say that we do need changes—but not complete cutoffs. There are people who sincerely need EBT. There are seniors struggling to make ends meet who could benefit from EBT simply because they don't have enough money to pay for the medicine they need and buy food on that fixed income. Unfortunately, the seniors—who have probably worked all their lives—wouldn't qualify for food stamps, while the younger person who keeps having babies to stay in the system would. I said it because we know it's true. That's where the system is broken. I believe that this system, without constant monitoring, has become a huge market for fraud.

These are the areas that can be modified to decrease the fraud that exists. Unfortunately, as funding is decreased for many of these programs, any form of monitoring the system for fraud and abuse is probably one of the first areas to be cut in the offices. Maybe the government shouldn't cut the oversight funding for these social programs. Monitoring them to cut out the fraud and abuse would mean huge savings for the government at the federal and state level.

Health care cost, Medicare, and Medicaid. Why is health care so expensive? If the cost for medical treatment is adjusted for those who are on Medicare/Medicaid, why isn't that the actual cost for everyone? Why are so many people being prescribed so much medication? I see people in my community who are taking up to 15 pills per day. I know this isn't what God had in mind for His creation.

It seems with all the advertisement of pills; we have resorted to taking a pill for everything. I understand many people don't go to the doctor regularly which sometimes put the person in an unfortunate situation when a problem is found. There are some illnesses and diseases that once a person is diagnosed, they are subjected to a lifetime of

59

prescription medicine. Diabetes is an excellent example. Is there a concept in the medical field whereby people who are classified as diabetics can be taught how they can rid themselves of that stigma? There should be.

There is a nutrition class most newly diagnosed diabetics are recommended to attend. Unfortunately, this class only teaches what you should and shouldn't eat. While that is good, the class or physician fails to tell the patient how to recover from being a diabetic. Not everyone can overcome diabetes, but some can.

Years ago, I was told I was a diabetic and I was given all kinds of prescriptions. After getting the prescriptions filled, I returned to work and took one of the pills, which made me nauseous. When I called the nurse practitioner, she advised me to take half the pill. I didn't take her advice. I went for a second opinion, which concluded I wasn't a diabetic at that time. At least ten years have passed and I'm now a diabetic. When the doctor wanted to put me on insulin, I said no. I asked him what I had to do to not go to insulin and eventually get rid of the diabetes. Lose weight was the first step. I did. I need to loose more, but the point here is that I didn't just accept what they said just because they said it. Sometimes, we need to challenge the decision of the medical personnel. The nurse practitioner was, in my opinion, pushing some new pills that were on the market at that time.

Unemployment Checks. Current recession and economic circumstances withstanding, how many people have used their unemployment benefits until they had maxed out, went back to work long enough to qualify for unemployment again, "lost" their job, and had to go on unemployment again? Our current situation makes things harder for people to get jobs. I understand that. However, there are many people who are cyclic recipients of unemployment. They have learned how to make the system work for them by doing what is necessary to get to continue on unemployment. How is it they can manage to keep their jobs just long enough to qualify for unemployment again and then, suddenly, they no longer have a job and must draw a check? I'm speaking only of those who are abusing the system.

For even when we were with you, we gave you this rule: "If a man will not work, he shall not eat." II Thessalonians 3:10

Is that really in the Bible? "If a man won't work, he won't eat"? Yes. God is certainly concerned about those less fortunate, but there is a difference between those less fortunate due to circumstances beyond their control and those who are simply lazy and/or unconcerned. Before you go off on a tangent, let me say that this isn't referring to any particular race of people. Rather, it's referring to the mindset of people who are content to be lifelong members of the welfare system. This thinking exists, to some degree, in all races. If the Bible is true, it also addresses laziness.

Lazy hands make a man poor, but diligent hands bring wealth. Proverbs 10:4

Based on this scripture as well as many others, our system shouldn't reward laziness. If our programs enable people to become addicted to this process, then that enabling needs to be changed. We shouldn't cut the entire program. There are people who are on unemployment now who never thought their lives would change so drastically. For many, it seems like a nightmare where they can't wake up. One important factor in this debate on jobs has to be how the Republicans are calling on the President to create jobs, yet they aren't doing anything to create jobs either. So how will we get the jobs created?

Diligent hands bring wealth. Having wealth is certainly not a sin. What people do with that wealth is where it becomes a problem in the spiritual sense. People often mistakenly say, "Money is the root of all evil." From a spiritual standpoint, the Bible makes clear what the real problem is concerning money.

> *For the love of money is a root of all kinds of evil. Some people, eager for money, have wandered from the faith and pierced themselves with many griefs.* I Timothy 6:10

It's not the money itself that's the problem, but the *love* of the money. When people love it so much that they take on a mindset of superiority and control as if they have become a god, it becomes dangerous for the person spiritually.

How can the "Christ-like" politician boldly uphold laws and legislature that defeat the well-being of the middle- and lower-class while feeding relentlessly to the already-rich? Greed for wealth and power is such a dangerous place to be for three reasons:

1) No man knows the day of his departure from this earth. Therefore, he should always be ready.

> *Moreover, no man knows when his hour will come: As fish are caught in a cruel net, or birds are taken in a snare, so men are trapped*

by evil times that fall unexpectedly upon them.
Ecclesiastes 9:12

2) Wealth won't profit a man's soul.

   *For what is a man profited, if he shall gain
   the whole world, and lose his own soul? Or
   what shall a man give in exchange for his
   soul?* Matthew 16:26 (KJV)

3) It is hard—but not impossible—for the rich to enter
   the Kingdom of God.

   *Then said Jesus unto his disciples, Verily I
   say unto you, that a rich man shall hardly
   enter into the kingdom of heaven. And again
   I say unto you, It is easier for a camel to go
   through the eye of a needle, than for a rich
   man to enter into the kingdom of God.*
   Matthew 19:23 (KJV)

For those of you who are rich, do the right thing—for your sake. Please stop supporting hate for our President with your wealth.

Chapter 9

Whose report will you believe?

If the Bible is true, who will you believe if you profess to be a Christian? You know the song *We'll Understand it Better By and By?* I love that God's Word is true, because I am having a "by and by" moment. I understand very simply, because I believe the Bible is true.

One day, we'll all have an unavoidable appointment with death, and when Judgment Day occurs, no one will be there to stand with or for us. We'll be on our own. All these people who are jumping to the words of others, falling for the lies, and hating because they have been taught to hate will have to try to come up with a justification to God in "hopes" that He will accept it. I have a secret! No clearance is needed. You will not be able to come up with one—if the Bible is true. Not only that, but you also won't be able to blame other people.

If the Bible is true and you are a real Christian and, therefore, Christ-like, you know the Bible.

Study to show thyself approved unto God, a workman that needeth not be ashamed, rightly dividing the word of truth. II Timothy 2:15 (KJV)

I believe this Scripture sums it up for the Christ-like. We are to study to be approved unto GOD, not man. We are to boldly—not shamefully—stand up for the Word of truth. These politicians who have no problem misrepresenting the truth must have decided it is better for them to be approved by a man at whatever cost than to be honorable in all his or her words and deeds.

As stated in the beginning, none of this is important if the Bible isn't true, and all I will have done is agitate a few people. But if there is at least one person who knows deep in their heart that they have had to misrepresent the truth to get elected—and found that what they thought would be of reward to them turned out to be to their detriment—then my writing is not in vain.

I believe President Obama has been appointed by God to hold this position "for such times as this." Unlike those who are saying the Lord told them or is telling them to run for office, President Obama hasn't made that claim. He doesn't have to. Those who support him and trust God even in a situation such as this understands who is really in charge. I also believe that those who have disrespected him, scandalized him, mocked him, and harbored hate towards him will have to come to repentance one day to be saved and receive the gift of eternal life—or not!

Everyone must submit himself to the governing authorities, for there is no authority except that which God has established. The authorities that exist have been established by God. Consequently, he who rebels against the authority is rebelling against what God has instituted, and those who do so will bring judgment on themselves. Romans 13:1-2

Do we really know what or who to believe in this jobs debate? From my observations, the truth isn't on the side of the Republicans. I don't say that because I'm a Democrat. Rather, I make that statement based on history.

Of great importance in this job debate is the emphasis that has been placed on tax cuts for small businesses to create jobs. I need help on this one.

The Republicans insist that if the taxes are raised for the millionaires and billionaires, there won't be any job creation. Well, if the Bush tax cuts have been in place for ten years and President Obama extended them in December 2010, why do we have a job crisis in the first place? Help me with this one. Who's the real culprit here? Based on the current Republican argument, when the Bush tax cuts were put in place, that should've given small businesses enough incentive to thrive. It's the Republicans who insist that raising taxes is a job killer. Apparently, cutting taxes is also a job killer. Is Old Man Greed playing in this game?

Just what happened to the jobs? I believe this is just a ploy—nothing more than a trick of the devil to convince people that President Obama must be defeated in 2012. It all goes back to the hatred that exists in this country by many, unfortunately, in high positions. But I'm just crazy enough to believe that as we make this deceit known, and as we uncover the real motives behind the deception constantly instigated by the Republicans and Tea Party, people will realize they have been misled.

67

With the Republicans being focused primarily on making certain President Obama doesn't get re-elected, will we see any job growth in the next year? What causes a company to hire more people? Demand for their product. If people don't have jobs and resources to buy the products, the jobs will not be created. This isn't about tax breaks. In fact, it's the working people who cause jobs to be created, not the millionaires and billionaires. When the working class has money to buy products, the demand increase and so do the jobs. Does that mean the Republicans push for lower taxes to create more jobs is simply made up?

After seeing firsthand what the elected Republicans have actually done to create jobs, I can't imagine why anyone in the less than $250,000 earnings category would consider voting for another. They campaigned on creating jobs, but they haven't passed one piece of legislature to create jobs. Why is that? They misled you. They scandalized President Obama to you with lies, and then they campaigned on jobs for you with lies. Their underlying, aggressive agenda is to make certain President Obama is a one-term president.

As the United States of America—the land of the free—we have to be better than this. Of all the criteria our elected officials should have, one should be direct accountability. This applies to the President as well. In doing so, we must make certain that the reasons for failure to meet standards are factual. We can't let a group of people tell us the President didn't create jobs when it's Congress who submits legislature to the President that would stimulate job growth. The Republicans have repeatedly criticized the President on his stimulus package—but what have they proposed to do to create jobs except provide tax cuts for the rich? The history of that proposal doesn't support that demand. What else do the Republicans have?

We can do better than this. Are there any politicians in Washington in the Republican Party who believe they can stand for all their people without being an active participant of operation "Let's make President Obama a one-term president"? Can you do your job honestly and trust the American people to make a decision on the President's performance, as well as the members of Congress when it's time for the next election?

Chapter 10

The American People
versus
The American People

Have you ever wondered who the American people are who are referenced by the politicians? They aren't the same group of people.

I am convinced by their drive, their commitment, and their emphasis that the American people referred to by the Republicans can only be the rich. There's no way the Republicans can be working for or concerned about the middle- and lower-income people. My evidence is based on the fact that the Republicans were willing to deny unemployment for thousands of people who were out of a job until they got an agreement to keep the tax cuts in tact for the millionaires and billionaires. They say they want to reduce the deficit, but they don't want to—and they refuse to touch the tax breaks for the rich and corporations. I would love to be a fly on the wall when that one has to be justified on Judgment Day.

Render therefore to all their dues: taxes to whom taxes are due, customs to whom customs, fear to whom fear, honor to whom honor. Romans 13:7 (NKJV)

On the other hand, I am also convinced by their drive, their commitment, and their emphasis that the American people referred to by most Democrats are all the people of the United States. My evidence is based on the fact that most Democrats were willing to support legislature that was portrayed as debt-increasing and unconstitutional by the Republicans and the Tea Party to help the middle and lower classes.

Let's refer back to health care reform. This bill was validated by the Congressional Budget Office (CBO) to decrease the deficit by trillions of dollars over a span of years. The Republicans and the Tea Party constantly misrepresented the honesty of the bill. We certainly don't want to forget Ms. "Death Panel" herself—such untrue words spoken for the sake of an election.

President Obama has been called many ugly and hateful names because he wants to help all people. He has attempted to bring about change that would benefit all people. I believe the American people that President Obama refers to encompasses everyone.

Is there any evidence that this issue with the Republicans isn't just about the President of today, but also Presidents of the future? Are we seeing evil run rampant through this country? For example, many organizations have been created to do anything and everything possible to stop the President from succeeding in anything. I believe when President Obama won the election, the opposing party conducted a thorough and very detailed study of which groups of people voted for him. Then they brainstormed how they could stop those groups of people from voting for President Obama in 2012. They didn't want to be honorable in the upcoming election. They just wanted to defeat the President—defeat him while he's in office by not passing anything that would benefit Obama's American people (everyone to include the rich). Under no circumstances could any member of Congress in the opposing parties support any legislation that would help the American people, thereby giving the President a positive outlook in office.

So, after they successfully created a monster of fear about President Obama, the people fell for the lies and hate and voted the "paid-for-by-the-rich" politicians into office. The intent was to have people in office who would undo everything that the President had done for Obama's American people so that the Republicans could make certain all legislatures would support the Republican American people (the rich ONLY).

It started with the labor union bills on collective bargaining in the states. If they can dissolve the unions, they can't organize and support the President. This one may backfire with viciousness in 2012 for the Republicans. The people are furious. Events in Wisconsin have been seen by people all over the United States. There are still some in the middle class who would rather vote against themselves than to see President Obama re-elected. Since the Republicans have elected many Republican Governors, the states are required to dissolve the labor unions. Collective bargaining is the main issue. Does that mean when the people of the states vote the Republicans in, they have no one to blame but themselves when their jobs and benefits start disappearing?

It moved to the voter registration changes. If they can make it harder to vote by making it harder to get registered, fewer people (Democrats and Independents) will be able to vote for President Obama. This means that you won't be able to show up the polls without proper ID to vote. Now in their view, many African-Americans and Hispanics will fail to get their IDs before Election Day. The devil is a liar, and the truth is not in him. If people understand the motives of these actions by the Republicans, that alone should get them fired up and ready to go—now!

Next step is the redistricting in the states. If they can change the zones in the states and make more of the blue zones red, they can change the previously predominately Democratic zones to Republican zones. In Wisconsin for example, the two Democrats who have been recalled for their districts will find themselves in a predicament because once they make it through the recall, they may have a residency issue. Because of the redistricting laws passed by the Governor, they may be living outside their districts.

Let's not forget the secret money. In the coming months of the 2012 campaign, we will see hate like we've never seen it before. When the Supreme Court allowed the raising of money by secret donors with no requirement for disclosure or even a limit to the amount, they opened up a gateway to evil and outright hatred the likes of which, again we've never seen before. This is one of the areas where the devil feels he really has control. Money can be used and is being used to support the hate loud and clear. If a person can support hate with no obligation of disclosure, the saying "Throw rocks and hide your hand" takes on a whole new meaning. Donors—beware. If the

Bible is true, every penny that is donated for hateful purposes will be an issue the donor will have to address.

To man belong the plans of the heart, but from the Lord comes the reply of the tongue. All a man's ways seem innocent to him, but motives are weighed by the Lord. Proverbs 16:1-2

The best of all is the immigration issues all over the United States. Having illegal immigrants working in plants and on farms used to be an excellent way for businesses to not have to pay high wages. The businesses didn't care whether they were legal. But the devil is always busy. It seems many legal Hispanics voted for President Obama in 2008. Therefore, being in this country illegally has taken on a whole new meaning. The Republicans are sending a message to the legal Hispanics that if their families come over here illegally, they'll send them back home. They won't let them work in their plants or on their farms anymore. States aren't going to support illegal immigrants in the workforce. The governors may be passing laws in every state to ban illegal immigrants. Of course laws have been in place before, but this time, they will be enforced.

Here is an excellent opportunity to show the hand of God.

Fret not thyself because of evildoers, neither be thou envious against the workers of iniquity. For they shall soon be cut down like the grass, and wither as the green herb. Psalm 37:1-2 (NKJV)

If the Bible is true, these evil, self-serving people who have bought the democracy of the United States Congress won't succeed as they think. They may make some headway and win a few battles. But because their means of operation are so deceitful, underhanded, and wrong, they will soon go away. They may win a few battles, but God is going to win the war.

Let me share some more evidence, if the Bible is true.

> *Finally, my brethren, be strong in the Lord, and in the power of His might. Put on the whole armour of God, that ye may be able to stand against the wiles of the devil. For we wrestle not against flesh and blood, but against principalities, against powers, against the rulers of the darkness of this world, against spiritual wickedness in high places.* Ephesians 6:10-12 (NKJV)

Where is the spiritual wickedness in high places? For this discussion, I believe it is definitely in some of the people in the Republican Party, the Tea Party and Congress.

Chapter 11

Privatization - Beware

This is a real wolf in sheep's clothing. Every time you hear a politician say ANYTHING should be privatized, shake your head and say NO. The Republicans would have you believe that Government shouldn't be involved in our day to day living. They would have you believe that it would be better to have private companies handling your personal affairs like health care, education and social security. I believe the reality is that if these areas are without any government oversight, the American people will be at the whim of some rich person or persons whose only motivation is greed.

What does it mean to privatize health care? It means you'll be subjected to the decisions of the insurance companies. If they don't want to pay your health bills, they won't. Why do you think the Republicans are pushing so hard to repeal the health care bill? I believe the main reason is that they don't want President Obama to have that victory under his belt. The insurance companies are paying millions of dollars to stop health care reform. Just like with the millionaires/billionaires who don't want to pay an increase in their taxes, the insurance companies would rather pay millions to keep from paying your benefits. They would pay someone good money to search your medical history to find something that would give them 'reason' to not pay your bills. Even if it isn't true, they may tell you they can't pay it. If you don't challenge them, they win. They know very few people will challenge them, so they win. Then if there is no government oversight on health care matters, rules have been deregulated so that the company can administer their programs the way they want, you would always be the loser.

Who benefits the most from privatized health care? The already-rich board members and, to a certain extent, the stockholders will reap the profits at the cost of your health. **Greed is such a dominate devil in our society.**

What does it mean to privatize education? It means your children may or may not get a good education. If all schools are private and you don't have the money to send your child to a private school, what happens? They'll get vouchers. Oh no—not Socialism! How can they allow a certain group of people control who is educated and who isn't? Not only that, wouldn't the privatization of education reintroduce segregation in the school systems? The best teachers would be hired in the best neighborhoods where the private schools are and the tuition would be higher. Children in low income households wouldn't be able to go to those schools. Therefore, while a low income family with a child may live near a community where the better private school is, that child would have to go miles further because of the tuition. Then, the schools would eventually begin to say what some doctor's say, "we aren't taking anymore Medicaid patients." Those schools will have some category identified that would allow them to discriminate against those children at any given time. We just can't let this happen. Many of our black children will simply fall by the wayside. Please don't think for one minute they'll care.

Most states have a lottery that was established to support education. Where is that money going? According to their websites, the following states have contributed lottery proceeds to education: Georgia – 12.5 billion, North Carolina – 2 billion, South Carolina 2.5 billion, Florida – 22 billion, and Virginia – 7.5 billion. If these resources are going to education, why are there proposals to cut education funding at the state and federal levels?

Who do you think will benefit from privatized education? The already-rich board members and, to a certain extent, the stockholders (if the option is available) are the ones who'll reap the profits at the cost of your future. **Greed doesn't care who he spits on.**

What does it mean to privatize Social Security? Wall Street!!! You'll be putting money into a system whereby someone else will invest your money in a stock, which may or may not prove profitable to YOU. You'll continue to contribute, and when it's time for you to retire, they'll simply say the market fell and that you have $100 left. If Social Security is privatized, thousands of investment firms will pop up and promise they'll invest and keep your investment secure. They'll lose your money and have to file bankruptcy or ask for a government bailout. They may get the bailout because the Republicans may have to support the investment firms since they were the ones who pushed for privatized Social Security. I have a few questions about privatized Social Security. What happens to the person who doesn't want to invest their money in one of those plans like an IRA or 401(k)? Will the 'government' force them to contribute? Will the money be automatically deducted from their pay? Would that requirement be considered 'unconstitutional' like the Republicans declare about the mandate in the health care bill? If a person doesn't invest and doesn't have a retirement account at age 65, who will take care of them? In all sincerity, the people who will come up short in privatized Social Security are the low income persons. The only way the rich would be affected would be if the stock market fell causing them to take a huge loss.

Who will benefit from privatized Social Security? Wall Street, the already-rich board members and, to a certain extent, the stockholders are the ones who'll reap the profits at the cost of your retirement. **Greed is a powerful carnal force.**

Then there is the term "big government." Let me let you in on a little secret. Do you have security clearance for this one? I believe the Republicans support big military (Department of Defense), but argue big government gets too much in our business. "Big military" encompasses so much. Have you ever wondered how many private contractors are doing what the military used to do and /or could do now? Do you know who some of these private contractors are? The majority of them are former politicians or former military personnel who have convinced their friends in the Department of Defense to award a contract to them and pay them huge bucks to do the tasks the military could do for a lot less. Let me state for the record that there is a "process" they have to go through to get the contract. You know that tank that isn't doing what it's supposed to do? Are we still paying for it? If so, is there an oversight problem in the management in the Department of Defense? They can't cut these private

80

contracts out because some "friend of a friend" helped a "friend of a friend" get the million-dollar contract. That "friend of a friend of a friend of a friend" relationship cannot be severed. The Department of Defense is a must for the Republicans NOT to cut.

Compare the money paid to private contractors versus an equivalent unit with much lower paid military personnel to do the same job and see how many MILLIONS would be saved. The Department of Defense and the Veteran's Administration (VA) don't have any problem recouping severance pay from veterans who have been out of the military for years and then start having health problems from service-connected disabilities. (NOTE: For all military getting out of service, if you are offered a severance pay, **don't take it** if you have had any illnesses or injuries while on active duty. You may regret it in later years when your health begins to decline, you are unable to work and you need to draw your compensation. They will care less whether or not you can survive.) Where does that money go that is recouped from veterans in need? The Veteran's Administration, from the state level (at least the VA in Columbia, South Carolina) to the national level, is so hard-nosed about this issue that they won't even consider asking Congress to authorize a monthly pro-rated amount for your severance recoupment to allow you to survive. Please don't take severance pay. Would the Department of Defense pay a contractor for products and/or services that don't meet the contract specification, but refuse to help a veteran in need? You betcha!

Who benefits from wars? Civilian contractors do. If President Obama brings the troops home as he said he would, many civilian contractors will be "up the creek." Who will they get their easy millions from? The

Republicans would have you believe that the money that's being directed to the Department of Defense cannot be touched, but your health care—and your life—can!

If the Bible is true, some of those "I want to be the greatest politician; therefore, I'll sell my soul to the devil" politicians are going to be in for a rude awakening on Judgment Day. **Greed will make a rich man cry.**

> *Why do you boast of evil, you mighty man? Why do you boast all day long, you who are a disgrace in the eyes of God? Your tongue plots destruction; it is like a sharpened razor, you who practice deceit. You love evil rather than good, falsehood rather than speaking the truth. You love every harmful word, O you deceitful tongue.* Psalm 52:1-4

Isn't God awesome? He inspired these men to write these Scriptures years ago about things that would be happening today. In giving us free will, He understood the shortcomings of His creation.

Chapter 12

A Real Solution for the
American People

Fire all the members of Congress. Get rid of every one of them. Hire 200 little old ladies and men to sit behind a desk with one or two representatives from each state. Let the Governors of each state submit proposals for laws and amendments at the national level on an annual basis. Allow all the proposals to be voted on in each state by the American people. The majority wins—end of story.

This would certainly cut down on the size of the government, as well as the cost. There would be no way these 200 people would get nearly as much compensation and benefits as the current Congress gets. Although they would be paid less, I believe they would be more efficient than the current Congress.

While this solution is not practical, the fact is the people who elected the Republicans and some Democrats have no say in what their representative does in Congress. Although they're supposed to represent the people in their state or district, why have the majority of Republicans signed an agreement with a man who is forcing them to do what he wants? The man may have power over the Republicans in Congress, but he doesn't have all the power.

I believe this is a great declaration of God being God in the midst of this situation. With all the issues the Republicans and Tea Party stirred up prior to the 2010 elections, there seems to be a reaping effect going on now. The fear factor was inflicted so that people would run to the polls to vote people in who would stop the President from "destroying" the United States. The Republicans put out so many lies to people who were susceptible to the fear factor. That became part of the justification for voting for so many Republicans. But now that the sheep's clothing has started to come off, the people are seeing wolves in the truth. I believe God is fed up with all the deceit that has been going on for years by Republicans and Democrats who are consistent with their lies and distortions for the sake of winning an election. If this is true, politicians should be more concerned about God's wrath than the man who had them sign the agreement to not raise taxes.

Giving an individual so much power that he can control the decisions of one side of the entire Congress has to be extremely dangerous. While that power may seem prestigious in this life, I wouldn't want to be in his shoes for anything in this world. I want to call your attention to the story of Lazarus and the unnamed rich man in the Bible. (Luke 16:19-31) That story didn't turn out well for the rich man.

When I was growing up, there was a story told by a

84

preacher about a rich man who thought he had more power than anyone, including God. There wasn't a biblical reference for this story, but it was used to make a point. The rich man wanted to challenge God. He would go to a high spot on his land and call God, challenging Him. The fact that God was not answering him made the man think he *was* more powerful than God. One day, after God had had enough of this foolish man, he sent a gnat—one of His tiny, annoying creations—to the man. The gnat flew into the man's throat and choked him to death. I guess you could say the man lost his power! Watch out for those gnats.

Governing the United States has to be an extremely hard job, but it doesn't have to be a nightmare. If the people who are elected to represent *all* the people—not just a select few—can't or won't do their jobs for the people who sent them to Washington, they should be removed. We need people in the government who aren't driven by power and greed to earnestly represent all the people of their district or state. To do anything less would be a failure on the part of the politician.

Congressman/Congresswoman consider a network system dedicated to only the people in your district. Every time there is an issue being considered in Congress, send an email out to all your constituents addressing the issue, legislature or bill. Explain to the people honestly what the bill represents. Open up a time period for discussion. Then close the discussion period and allow each constituent to vote on the issue. Let the votes be available for view by a constituent number. Once the votes are complete, see where the people really stand. The results of that vote from your constituents in your district/state should be how *you* actually vote. Do that and I would certainly call you a politician truly representing all the people in your district/state. But we know the Republicans would never do that because they would run the risk of having to go against the wishes of their constituents to support the demands of the lobbyists and anyone else with whom they are in bed.

Here's a budget cut that could put millions on the table: Ask every member of Congress to agree to a pay cut of 50% of their current salary. Most of them are millionaires. Let's see some "love my country and my people" mindsets negotiate this at the table.

The next time your representative is up for election, ask him or her exactly who they represent. Ask them if they have any agreements with any agency or person who doesn't have anything to do with them being in office representing you. Ask them if they are in bed with the lobbyist to the point of sacrificing your future to meet the objectives of the lobbyists. Ask them if they are willing to stand up for their voters even if it means the voters don't necessarily agree with the other members of Congress. Ask them if they can be trusted to do the right thing for everyone and not just a select few.

Please—to any reader who'll actually think about what the Republicans are doing to sabotage the progress in this country, think about this at election time. Until the haters and obstructionists are voted out, people will have to take a serious look at what these people are saying. Will you be able to believe what they say? They have proven beyond a shadow of a doubt that they cannot be trusted. Ask the questions. Don't sit back and act shocked after the elections when the things they campaigned ON—jobs, jobs, jobs—fall short because of who they are working FOR—rich, rich, rich.

On Friday, July 8, 2011, the unemployment rate went up to 9.2. As I listened to the comments from both sides of Congress, I was amazed. Back in January 2011, when the unemployment rate went down, the Republicans took credit for the decrease. But now that it's gone back up, it's President Obama's fault. According to the Republicans, the only way the jobs are going to come back is if taxes are lowered. I don't get this. Congressman Eric Cantor said we can't raise taxes on the small businesses and families. This is not what President Obama is saying. Let's set that lie aside for a moment. If lowering taxes would create jobs, I ask again, "Why did the jobs decrease in the first place?" The taxes have been low for the past ten years—so why have we lost jobs? This is why I believe it's all about the hate of this President and the fact that the Republicans will say whatever they have to in order to prevent President Obama from being re-elected.

Those of you who have actually read this book—consider the consequences if you harbor any hate for President Barack Obama. If you honestly think he is anything but a serious man who honestly wants to help ALL the American people, pray for him. Ask God to help him make right decisions that will be a blessing to all citizens. Pray for yourself. Ask God to remove any wrongly harbored feelings towards the President that may cost you at His judgment. Pray for peace in our country. Pray for brotherly love for everyone. Pray that our country will thrive and be prosperous, and that all of God's people will know Him and the promises that He made to all of us.

There is a call for prayer in Texas by Governor Perry in August. On the surface, this seems to be a good thing—but I question his motives. From a quote by Governor Perry:

"Given the trials that beset our nation world, from the global economic downturn to natural disasters, the lingering danger of terrorism and continued debasement of our culture, I believe it's time to convene the leaders from each of our United States in a day of prayer and fasting, like that described in the book of Joel." He said this in a written statement.

"I urge all Americans of faith to pray on that day for the healing of our country, the rebuilding of our communities, and the restoration of enduring values as our guiding force."

Governor Perry is calling for the leaders of each state to come for a day of prayer and fasting as found in the book of Joel. I read the book of Joel to understand the Governor's purpose, and I think he left out a key element—a call for repentance. Praying and fasting is good, but repentance is a must.

"Now therefore," says the Lord, *"Turn to Me with all your heart, With fasting, with weeping, and with mourning." So rend your heart, and not your garments; Return to the Lord your God, For He is gracious and merciful, slow to anger, and of great kindness; And He relents from doing harm.* Joel 2:12-13 (NKJV)

The word is clearly calling for repentance. We can't turn *to* God until we turn *from* our wicked ways.

If my people who are called by my name will humble themselves, and pray and seek my face, and turn from their wicked ways, then I will hear from heaven, and will forgive their sin and heal their land. II Chronicles 7:14 (NKJV)

God's Word is trustworthy. He can be counted on every time. He calls us to repentance first. Praying and asking God to heal our land, but not being willing to turn from our wicked ways, is like calling for a deficit reduction with spending cuts and not calling for revenue increases. Not only is it not right, but it will not solve the problem.

I realize by the time this book is published, the day of prayer will be over and hopefully, the debt ceiling debate will also be resolved—hopefully. Unfortunately, there will be some other drawn out issue that Congress will be arguing about instead of getting things done in a timely and productive basis. How many people in the real world would still have their jobs if they were as ineffective and argumentative as our current Congress? These people are paid good money to create havoc in our government.

Well, the day of prayer is over and the Governor has launched his campaign. He prayed on Saturday and began the personal attack on Sunday! See that's why repentance wasn't a part of his call for prayer. He knew he was going to stir up mess for the sake of trying to win an election. When he was challenged on some of the things he said, he initially did not back down. But after a few days of being criticized by members of his party, he changed his tone. TOO LATE. I believe what he said and how he acted during the first 24-48 hours after declaring his run for President was the real man. This is how he would be as President of the United States. He used many of the fear 'buzz' words: need a President that loves this country, need a President that is respected by the military. To make comments as such implies the opposite of the current President. That is inciting hatred. Just because a few members of his party were able to get him to tone his arrogance down doesn't change the fact that he was comfortable being that way because he is who you saw and heard.

We sing a song in church that says:

Search me, Lord. Shine the light from Heaven on my soul. If you find anything that shouldn't be, take it out and strengthen me. I wanna be right, I wanna be saved, I wanna be whole.

From this song, I would add the following in a prayer request for our nation.

Search us, Lord. When you find the things in our hearts that don't please you, take them out. Remove them and cast them into the sea of forgetfulness. Perform a transformation in our minds that coincides with your Word to be transformed by the renewing of our minds. We pray for our nation as a whole. We strive to be the leader of the free world. Lord, bring us to a place of leading in the love that you request of us. Help us to be a people of forgiveness, a people of love, a people of joy. Bring us together in healing. We are but filthy rags in your site. We call on you to forgive us collectively and individually of our sins, both of commission and of omission. We pray for your forgiveness of our sins against you and against others. Help us to seek your guidance daily as the forefront of what we set out to do. Loose our hearts from the hatred that exists in this nation that the devil will not have victory in our lives or become a stumbling block for anyone.

We pray for the leaders of this country. We pray for cooperation with one another among those who have been elected to be stewards over the governance of this nation. Help them to see you. Let this be the year that "King Uzziah" dies so that we will see you high and lifted up. Let this be the season that all focus will be on you, that you'll be exalted and glorified.

We call out greed in the name of Jesus. We call out hatred in the name of Jesus. We call out sexual immorality in the name of Jesus. We call out deceit in the name of Jesus. We call out jealousy in the name of Jesus. We call out pride in the name of Jesus. We call out anything that is not in your will that it will be destroyed in our lives to allow total commitment to you and your will. In the name of Jesus, we petition you and your glory for such a time as this. For such a time as man will hurt others for personal gain. For such a time as man will neglect their call to serve you.

We honor you, Lord, for giving us grace and mercy instead of what we deserve. We lift you in glory, adoration, and praise. Thank you, Lord, for everything you have done for the United States of America. Even when we didn't understand why things were happening, we knew by faith that you were still in control. You are our provider, our Prince of Peace. Reign over these United States that men will know you in the pardoning of their sins. For these things we ask in Jesus' name. Amen.

I applaud the one person who, after reading this book, acknowledges that they have listened to ungodly counsel and, as a result, harbored hatred towards the President. For this one person—if the Bible is true—who has recognized and repented, on Judgment Day, this person will hear the words: "Well done, thy good and faithful servant."

To God be the glory for the things He has done!

God bless you, and God bless the United States of America.

Chapter 13

On a Lighter Note – to the President

Mr. President, I salute you for all the things you have done and tried to do during your first administration. I love the way you and your family keep going despite the constant hate and put-downs. I believe that when it's all said and done, you'll ask God not to hold their irresponsible words, deeds, and feelings toward you personally against them. That's the way I see you.

The people are constantly trying to trip you up, but you're smart. You're witty, and I'm certain there have been times you would've liked to tell them a thing or two. I have no doubt they've been trying desperately to get you to react in a hostile manner. But you always maintained your honorable demeanor.

Since the Republicans are against everything you are for, even if they were for it before they were against it, do you think you could get a bill through by reverse psychology? LOL

Hang in there Mr. President, your work isn't in vain.

There's just one issue, however, that I would like to share with you. Not many African-American people say "the fact of the matter is." While this may be politically correct, just once I'd love to hear you make this statement the old-fashioned way: matta fact. Not matter of fact, but matta fact. ☺

As stated in the dedication, my mother was very proud of you. She would get upset when the people would give you a hard time. But she knew you could handle the situation with the utmost respect.

We love you, President Obama and First Lady. May God bless and protect you always.

ATTENTION
OBAMA
HATERS:

What if the Bible is true?
Will your hate of this man be worth the price
you may have to pay?

Annette Boyd Lee is the author of the book,
When Words Hurt.

Published in 2011, the book was inspired by God and the old saying, 'sticks and stones may break my bones, but words will never hurt me.' *When Words Hurt* is the first of five books portraying the struggles people often deal with as a result of the harsh words of others. Annette Lee skillfully portrays three families whose children experience disappointment and heartaches at the voice of someone else, usually an adult. The stories will exemplify God's presence in the least of them to bring about a change that will benefit not only the children but the adults as well. Readers will share their heartaches and celebrate with them as they share in the fulfillment of their desires. *When Words Hurt* is a perfect tool for teens and parents of teens to learn how to understand, appreciate, and follow the call to seek God first in their lives.

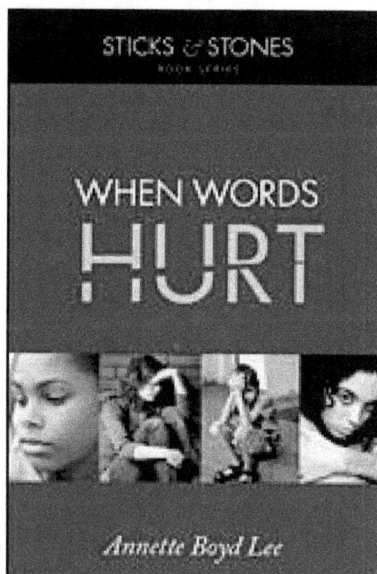

For more information, to include the first chapter, testimonials, more about the author and instructions for obtaining an autographed copies, please go to www.sticksandstonesbookseries.com

Also, available at Amazon.com and Barnes&Noble.com.

Author Contact Information:

Annette Boyd Lee
P.O. Box 442
Clinton, SC 29325

Website: www.booksbyannette.com

Email: miebenezer@aol.com

For speaking engagements, conferences or seminars, please complete the contact form at the following link:

http://booksbyannette.com/contact.htm

Just imagine all the assets that you can bring to the market world when you bring out what God has placed in you.

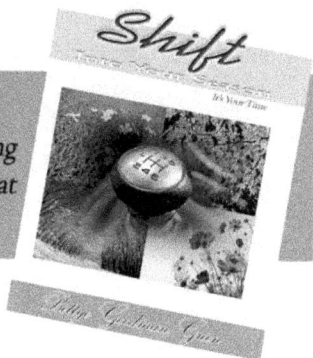

Shift
It's Your Time

There is no greater time than now to shift into your season. Do you feel as if time is running out? If so, then this is the book you need! Shift Into Your Season is inspiration, life and passion at its best! If you are one of the 7,000,000 baby boomers, you may feel like it's too late to accomplish your goals...as if God can't use you now. Think again!

This book challenges you to tap into those hidden talents that have yet to be discovered. Just think of all the assets that you carry into the world of marketing when you bring out what God has placed in you. You may have been delayed but not denied. It's not too late to shift into your season!

Bettye Green is an Author, Motivational Speaker and Evangelist. She resides in New Bern, NC with her husband/Pastor and is a loving mother, grandmother and great grandmother. In the fall season of her life, she shifted into a change of career and began working in the Corporate World as her co-workers were retiring. Her multi-educational background allowed her to earn degrees that were needed to make the shift and to accomplish her goal in this season of her life.

Bettye Green, Author
Email: author.bettye1@yahoo.com
P.O. Box: 14092 New Bern NC 28561
Website: www.jasherpress.com
Contact Number: 252.638.5525